Letters to Myself
Volume 2
Sexual Assault, Rape, & Incest

By:
Award Winning
&
#1 International Bestselling Author
Jen Taylor, LCSW

ELITE PUBLISHING
HOUSE
YOUR LEGACY. YOUR BOOK.

First Edition

Copyright 2024 © Jen Taylor, LCSW

All Rights Reserved

No part of this book may be reproduced or transmitted in any form or by any means, electronic or mechanical, including photocopying, recording or by an information storage and retrieval system – except by a reviewer who may quote brief passages in a review to be printed in a magazine, newspaper or on the Web – without permission in writing from the publisher.

Photo Credits: Dalia Adl

Cover Graphics: Kathryn Denhof

To those of us who had our innocence taken from us and were violated without our consent...may we continue to heal...

UNITED STATES:

If you or someone you know is experiencing sexual assault, rape, or incest - please reach out 24/7 to the following:

National Sexual Assault Hotline:
800 656 HOPE or www.rainn.org
(Rape, abuse, and incest national hotline)

National Domestic Violence Hotline:
800 787 7233 or www.thehotline.org

Planned Parenthood Hotline:
800 230 7526 or www.plannedparenthood.org

TABLE OF CONTENTS

FOREWORD 8
Paula Eberling

INTRODUCTION 12

COLLECTION OF LETTERS 16
J
Jen Taylor
Jessica Newell
Guinevere Smith
Anonymous
Keya-di
Jen Taylor
Anonymous

MESSAGES OF HOPE 53
Unedited Messages of Hope

APPENDIX ON SUPPORT RESOURCES & CHOICES 55
Includes Links, Numbers, & Resources for Sexual Assault, Rape, Incest, and Pregnancy Choices
Jen Taylor, LCSW

APPENDIX ON SUICIDE RESOURCES 57
Includes Resources for Suicide Help & Assessment

CONDUCT A SUICIDE INQUIRY 70

DETERMINE RISK LEVEL 73

ABOUT THE AUTHOR 75

FOREWORD

THE RIPPLING EFFECT OF SEXUAL CRIME
Paula Eberling
Social Justice Advocate,
Survivor, Speaker, & Bestselling Author

Moving from victim to survivor is a daunting journey. For some, healing from trauma is a lifelong process that doesn't always have a happy ending.

For myself, becoming a survivor of child sexual abuse, molestation, sexual assault, rape, and sex trafficking, has truly been a lifelong journey. I became a victim of sexual abuse at the of three. My abusers groomed and conditioned me to become the perfect victim.

My childhood home was filled with violence. My siblings and I were disciplined through fear, and obedience was a learned trait that followed me through my adolescence and adulthood.

I became an easy target for anyone who saw my longing to be loved at any cost. Cheating boyfriends and abusive boyfriends became a repeating pattern for me. At the age of fourteen, I used alcohol to numb myself. I ran away multiple times, which landed me in a group home for troubled teens.

That was the christening for my first experience of being sold for sex. I was a compliant victim. My conditioning as a child brought my body to a familiar place. If I were a good girl, I would survive.

I married at the age of 17 to escape my life. I had dreams of living a normal, happy life. I didn't see the beast before me. Domestic violence encapsulated me fully. Once again, I became obedient and merely existed to survive. I stayed in the marriage for eighteen years. Escaping the only life I had known seemed impossible and dangerous. The departure nearly took my life, and it took me ten years to find peace without guilt.

Years of abuse had left me empty and feeling like I couldn't do anything right. I felt worthless and didn't think that I deserved anything but misery. I blamed myself. The recovery process required re-living the abuse.

Moving from victim to survivor was the most challenging step in recovery for me. It took years of counseling and acknowledging my worth to overcome the trauma caused by others. I am no longer held hostage by the past.

Jen Taylor's book allows survivors to share their voices. Sexual abuse, rape, and incest are too often silenced. Sharing traumatic experiences provides a platform of healing and awareness while becoming the lighthouse for others to follow in hopes that they, too, can start the healing journey.

Letters to Myself creates a ripple effect that reaches many. Thank you, Jen, for creating the platform that offers hope to those affected by sexual trauma.

> *"I alone cannot change the world, but I can cast a stone across the water to create many ripples."*
>
> — **Mother Teresa**

PAULA EBERLING
SOCIAL JUSTICE ADVOCATE
SURVIVOR   SPEAKER
BEST SELLING AUTHOR
ENTREPRENEUR

Paula is a recognized social justice advocate, speaker, trainer, survivor and leader in the movement to end modern-day slavery and human trafficking.

Paula served as the Director of the Seventh Judicial Victim Witness Program for twelve years and has 26+yrs experience as a victim's advocate, humanitarian and human rights activist. She passionately advocates for the services, resources, awareness and social reform of victims' rights.

Retirement brought new adventures for Paula. In 2021, she purchased a local ice-cream shop and soon thereafter added coffee and assorted pastries to the menu. Paula prides herself on employing area youth to empower them by teaching them valuable skills and how to give back to their community.

Paula has personally overcome sex trafficking, child sexual abuse, domestic violence, psychological abuse and sexual assault. Through her healing experience, she has become a whistle-blower/ change maker of the justice system, a voice for empowering survivors across the globe.

Her experiences in life makes her an excellent liaison, bridging the gaps in the system, guiding individuals to various resources, and advocate for all people.

In her talks she openly shares her healing journey and how the traumas in her life became her biggest blessings.

Leadership
- Founder & Facilitator of the Eastern Montana Human Trafficking Task Force
- Founder of the Survive to Thrive Virtual Support Group and partnering Workbook
- Advocate
- Graduate of Leadership Montana 2017 class
- Graduate of Leadership Montana 2019 Masters class
- Certified Mediator
- Certified Trauma Support Specialist
- Victim Witness Specialist
- Former Certified Nursing Assistant
- Former Program Director of 7th Judicial Victim Witness Program
- Paralegal
- Mother, Grandmother, Wife
- Small Business Owner
- Best Selling Author

You can't make a change if you're not at the table. Join me, *Paula Eberling*

CONNECT WITH PAULA

EMAIL: pneberling@gmail.com
PHONE: 406-480-4676
WEBSITE: www.paulaeberling.com
FACEBOOK: @SurviveToThrive

INTRODUCTION

Rape is often misunderstood. It is actually a violent crime that is acted out through a sexual act, not a sexual act in and of itself.

Dictionary.com defines rape as follows:

"Unlawful sexual intercourse or any other sexual penetration of the vagina, anus or mouth of another person, with or without force, by a sex organ, other body part, or foreign object, without the consent of the person subjected to such penetration."

There are many myths surrounding rape. I would like to address two of these. Firstly, that the victim is usually female, and secondly, that one "asks for it" in some way by agreeing to engage in foreplay with the rapist or by wearing clothing that is considered "inappropriate or seductive." According to NSVRS, 91% of rape survivors are women, while 9% are male.

In some cultures, and countries, "rape" is allowed and not criminalized in a marriage; the male partner is allowed legally to have sex with their partner without consent because they are married. In some countries, genital mutilation still occurs, which precludes pleasure or orgasm for the woman.

From personal and professional experience, one of the hardest emotional parts of surviving sexual abuse is the shame, guilt, and self-blame. In trauma, the mind often needs a reason for the traumatic event, even if it is not true or doesn't make sense. In this case, the mind blames the survivor so that it can "file away" the experience in a category in an effort to make sense of it. I have found John Bradshaw's work incredibly helpful in my own healing process, both as a survivor of rape and as an ACOA (adult child of an alcoholic.) *Healing the shame that binds you* is incredibly life-affirming and helpful in releasing and healing shame. EMDR is a wonderful therapeutic trauma and EFT technique (tapping); see Brad Yeats on YouTube.

Statistics:

NSVRS - National Sexual Violence Resource Center: 91% of rape victims are women. 9% are male. In 8 out of 10 rapes, the victim knows the rapist. In January of 2024, Governor Kathy Hochul of New York redefined the law under the name "rape is rape," removing the requirement of penetration in the definition. "Our new law redefines rape as non-consensual vaginal sexual contact as well as non-consensual oral and anal sexual contact protecting LGBTQ people and others…"

Rape is responsible for many mental health disorders for its survivors. PTSD, post-traumatic stress disorder, initially used for those witnessing or participating in active combat, also affects survivors of rape, sexual assault, incest, and other traumas. 80% percent of survivors will experience one mental health issue, while 50% percent of survivors will experience two.

50% of women and 30% of men will experience sexual assault in their lifetimes. "Young women are in the highest risk category for sexual violence. The highest risk years are between the ages of 12 and 34. Girls aged 16-19 are four times more likely than any other demographic to be rape or sexual assault victims." - Charliehealth

80% of rape survivors know their perpetrator.

Resources:

National Sexual Assault Hotline: 800 656 HOPE
or www.rainn.org
(Rape, abuse, and incest national hotline)

National Domestic Violence Hotline: 800 787 7233
or www.thehotline.org

Planned Parenthood Hotline: 800 230 7526
or www.plannedparenthood.org

If you'd like to reach out to me:
jentaylorfani@gmail.com
212-470-3280

COLLECTION OF LETTERS

At the age of 8, my life changed dramatically. I went from a book-reading, Star Trek-living, Nintendo-playing girl to a girl who was violated by someone she trusted, someone her parents trusted. The little girl that once was did not realize the impact that one moment would have on her life. What started as an innocent game of hide & seek with an older brother and a (sort of brother) turned into the sort of brother touching and rubbing against her in a way that she immediately knew was wrong. Maybe not to what extent, but she got nauseous and was terrified. She started to cry, jumped up, and ran into her room. When her parents got home, it took her a day or so, but she told them what happened and was told she was mistaken. This person would never do that. She was his little sister. It hurt even more that she was not believed, especially about something so serious. Due to this, this was not the last time she was left with him. That was the only time he ever touched her in that way, but it was not the last time he put her in an inappropriate situation. As this little girl got older, she realized she had major issues with substance abuse. But that did not excuse the damage it did. It also wasn't the last time she was violated in such a way.

But through prayer and lots of therapy, she has been able to move past the pain. She will never forget, but it will never again define her or her worth.

The girl is me, and I am healing ♥

- J

I was a freshman in college, and there was a guy I liked - named Areen - who lived at the Black Cultural Center. He invited me to a party, and I accepted. I was excited to fool around but wasn't ready for anything more. I had had sex for the first time in high school with my first love, but I really didn't know this guy too well.

We had met in the pool room - where I spent much of my freshman year - when I wasn't reading Hegel and Heidegger for my philosophy major.

We went to a party at La Casa - the Spanish cultural center a little bit off campus. He shared a joint with me – I had never smoked, so I coughed a lot and got a little high. He brought me back to his room, and we started kissing. We got to third base, but I wasn't ready for more. I told him I didn't have any birth control, and he insisted. He didn't listen. He came inside me. I was shocked and went into the bathroom to try to wash him out of me.

A few weeks later, on my reserve weekend for the Navy, I noticed my jeans felt tighter, and I couldn't close the button. When I returned to campus, I asked my best friend, Agnes, to come with me to the pharmacy for a pregnancy test. They were expensive. I used the bathroom on her floor, and yes, I was pregnant. And he was the only guy. I cried and hugged my friend. I didn't realize that I had been date raped. I called my mom and eventually went home and terminated the pregnancy. I couldn't tell her what happened. I lied and said it was an accident. I was so ashamed.

I ran into him weeks later in the pool room. I tried to avoid conversation. He asked where I'd been. He already knew. My friend, Tommy, told me that Areen did this intentionally to white women. It was his form of payback.

And what I lost with that experience was my carefreeness, my happiness, a fetus I never wanted.

I can share my story now without shame. It was not my fault. That was a date. I was raped on a date – something that took me so long to understand and realize that I had no fault in.

It is not what we wear or how we talk - we don't "ask for it."

Rape is a violent crime whose vehicle is sex.

Don't be ashamed.

Get help.

Talk to a friend or a trusted adult or therapist.

Go to a clinic like Planned Parenthood.

No means no.

My kids and I talk about sex, STDs, pregnancy, rape, and consent.

Thank you for witnessing my story.

Planned Parenthood:
800 230-7526
Plannedparenthood.org

Sexual Assault Hotline USA:
8006 4673

- Jen Taylor

I was fifteen years old when I met Tyler. I was dealing with the aftermath of my suicide attempt and bullying, so I was very vulnerable. He was five years older than me, but that didn't matter to me at the time.

In December 2013, I had just turned sixteen, and Tyler asked me to be his girlfriend. Initially, I was hesitant, but he promised he would love, take care of, and cherish me. So, I agreed to date him. Looking back at it now, I realize who I was at the time, and everything I had gone through was the reason who wanted to be with me. I was naïve, young, and in desperate need of someone to like me. He liked me, loved me, and even told me constantly how much he cared for me. How he would never hurt me, never leave me. For the first year of our relationship, he kept his word. He was a good guy. He was nice to me. He paid attention to me; he complimented me, he was there for me when I needed someone. In my eyes, he was my knight in shining armor.

It started with just verbal and emotional abuse. He would make comments about my weight, how stupid I was, and how I always messed things up. He would tell me that I was worthless, that no one would love me the way he did, that I was lucky he wanted me. He controlled everything I did. He never liked the way I dressed or the way I had my hair. He didn't like it when I made plans with my friends without asking if it was okay with him first. He wouldn't let me come over to his house if his friends were there because he didn't want me to flirt with them. I had to show him my phone whenever we were together. He had to approve my outfits, phone calls, hangouts, and text messages. Everything had to go through him first; if it didn't, he got mad.

The first time he hit me, I was seventeen. I was at his house, and he told me he was hungry, so I needed to make something for him. When I brought him the food, he tasted it and didn't like it. He threw the plate past my head, and it shattered against the wall. I had no idea what to do, so I just mumbled an apology. He grabbed my arm and shook me a bit. He was screaming about how I couldn't do anything right, and that's when he slapped me. I was frozen. The pain in my cheek slowly grew, and the fear in my mind took over my body. I couldn't move; I didn't know how to. That made him angrier. He grabbed my arm again and shoved me towards the broken plate on the ground. He picked up the pieces and said it was my fault, that if I hadn't made him mad, if I had just done it right the first time, then this wouldn't have happened. He told me to clean up my mess and come find him when I finished. He hugged me, kissed my forehead, and told me if I behaved from now on, it wouldn't happen again.

I won't lie; I held a small bit of hope that he was telling me the truth. I knew that it wouldn't happen again and that everything would be fine if I were better and a good girl. The flicker of hope got smaller and smaller every day. It didn't matter how hard I tried to be good enough; it was never good enough for him. Everything I did made him upset. He would punch, slap, kick, pull my hair, choke me no matter what I did. He would threaten me, and he was going to kill me if I left him. He was going to hurt my family if I told anyone. He made sure I kept my mouth shut. I would lie to my friends about the bruises. I was good at lying about myself and had plenty of practice. I was good at faking a smile and not letting anyone know the truth.

I was eighteen years old when he raped me. I was at his house, we were watching a movie, and he asked me to get him a glass of water. I quickly got up from the couch and sprinted to the kitchen to get it. I didn't want to keep him waiting for fear that he might hit me if it took too long. I came back and sat the glass down on the coffee table in front of the couch. I looked at him and asked if I could go to the bathroom. He laughed, kissed my head, and said, "Sure, baby." When I came back, he resumed the movie. A few minutes went by; he reached down to grab the water; as he was about to take a sip, he stopped. He handed the glass to me, and instinctively, I flinched a bit when I saw his hand coming towards me. He asked if I wanted to drink some, and I said no and set my focus back to the movie; he grabbed my face and said, "Drink now," very firmly. I nodded my head and opened my mouth as he made me drink the water. He patted my head and told me I was a good girl.

I woke up the next morning naked, in his bed, and in a lot of pain. My head was pounding, my body felt numb and tingly, my ears were ringing, and my vision was blurry. I couldn't remember anything. The last thing in my mind was drinking the water, watching the movie, and then feeling sleepy.

Tyler wasn't there. I got up and stumbled my way toward the bathroom, picking up what I assumed were my clothes along the way. I washed my face in the sink and took a moment to try and collect myself. I walked back to the bedroom to try and find my phone. I noticed the bed sheet had blood on it. I started to panic. I thought I had started my cycle, and I was scared. If Tyler finds out I got blood on his sheets, I'm in trouble. I made the decision to change the sheets before he came back; if he didn't know, I would be safe. I was just about to grab the corner of the sheet when I heard a ding come from his computer. I went towards the computer to see what it was; he had gotten an email from someone. I reached out to check it and then stopped, a thought popping into my head. If he finds out you looked at his computer without his permission, you know what will happen. I stood there weighing the options in my mind until I heard another ding. He had gotten another email from the same person. Maybe it's important then; maybe he won't get mad if I look at it for him. I opened the email, and it felt like my entire world exploded. It was a video, a video that he had recorded of him raping me, and he had sent it to a friend of his. He was bragging about it, going on and on to his friend about what he had done and how amazing it made him feel, knowing he owned me now, that I was completely his.

I couldn't breathe, I couldn't think. Everything was moving in slow motion. Nothing made sense anymore. I couldn't fathom how someone could do something so monstrous. He was a monster, a monster I couldn't escape from. I couldn't stop myself from crying. I cried and cried for what felt like hours. I didn't know what to do, so I called a friend to come pick me up. I needed to leave. I needed to get out of this room, out of this house. When she got there, I ran to her car and told her just to drive. She asked me what was wrong, but all I could manage to get out was, "Take me to the Health Department." She didn't question me, she didn't pry any further, she just did what I asked. She went in with me, waited for me to finish, and drove me to her house afterward. When I told her what happened, she tried to convince me to report him, but I was petrified. The threats he made crept up in the back of my mind. She managed to persuade me to give her Tyler's mother's phone number. She called her and told her, with my permission, what her son had done. She told his mom that she would report him, and his mom said she would handle it. He was arrested about a month later. His mom said that they found a lot of other videos of other girls he had done this to, and because of the amount of evidence they had, Tyler's lawyer told him to take a plea deal. He was sentenced to 10 to 15 years in prison.

I spent three and a half years with a man I once thought was my savior. He blindsided me into thinking it was love. He used me, tortured me, broke me, and turned me into someone I didn't even recognize. He convinced me I was alone, that no one would believe me, that I was better off with him. He made me believe he was my only option, the only one who truly loved me. He stole my heart, my confidence, my body, and my soul. He took everything he could from me and never apologized for it. I blamed myself for what happened to me. I told myself it was my fault, that I was the reason for all this. If I had just been a little stronger. If I had just been smarter. If I had told someone. If I had been a little braver. With all these ifs and buts, you slowly start to hate yourself. You hate yourself for what you allowed them to do to you. You hate yourself for not being able to protect yourself. You hate yourself for not being able to fight back. You direct all your anger toward yourself. You mentally beat yourself up. You treat and see yourself the way they did because you genuinely believe you deserve it.

I am NOT to blame for the bruises on my body and soul.
I am NOT to blame for the innocence that was taken from me.
I am NOT to blame.
I AM worthy of genuine love and affection.
I AM allowed to be scared and emotional at the same time as being brave and steady.
I AM good enough.

"I'm worth being committed to. I refuse to let anybody make me feel as if I am less deserving than another. I will no longer allow anybody to fill my eyes with tears or waste my valuable time if they are not willing to see what a great woman is standing in front of them. It's not my responsibility to fix someone's way of thinking, so if I feel like I deserve better...I'll do better."

~ M. Sosa, The Mistakes of a Woman - Vol. 1 ~

I wish I could tell you it gets better, but that wouldn't be truthful. The trauma and the mark it has left on you will most likely always be there. It will affect you; it will alter you. That doesn't mean you can't heal from it. You can heal as long as you choose to. It doesn't get better; you do.

"I think there is a pressure on people to turn every negative into a positive, but we should be allowed to say, 'I went through something really strange and awful, and it has altered me forever."

~ Marian Keyes ~

- Jessica Newell

Not a Wife's Duty

Sex with you was never loving
It was demanding and selfish
Expected at best
Take one for the team
I was taught and encouraged.

Afraid to lay in my own bed
Scared to fall asleep
Surely, you would find yourself on top of me
With no regard for my feelings
Trust shattered, and didn't even realize.

I was jumpy
I was scared
I couldn't share my feelings
They would be used against me
I lived in constant fear

One particular day, you outwardly raped me
I said NO.
I would serve him with divorce papers
He would take that chance
What?!
Then held me down.

People didn't seem to understand
Took one for the team, huh?
That is your wifely duty

I'd like to say it didn't happen again
But it did
He was losing control of his wife

I was beginning to stand up for myself
I was asking questions
Demanding answers and respect
You will lose me

You never cared about me
You never loved me
You continued to just climb on top of me
Even when I slept on the couch
You thought you were claiming me as yours

I was never yours
You didn't love me
Not the way I deserved
Not the way I demand and expect now

Now I teach girls about guys like you
I left you so my girls didn't find a jerk like you
And my son would never treat his wife like that
It wasn't normal
It is not okay

I am whole again
Without you…..

- Guinevere Smith

I was five.
Five.
It had been a horrible year.
My grandpa had passed over suddenly.
Our apartment had a fire, and we had to live in a hotel for several months.
The hotel was on West 57th Street
It was there that my life would be forever changed.

It was a winter evening, and my parents were asleep in the bedroom.
Two of my brothers and I slept in the living room on single beds.
John was sleeping, but Ian was awake.
Ian beckoned me toward him and told me to give him a hand job
He told me I would get in big trouble if I ever told anyone.
I did what he asked, scared and with a sick feeling in my belly...because I knew it wasn't something a brother should be asking his sister to do.
Especially his little sister.
I never felt safe with him again.
I felt my parents and John had failed to protect me.
Even my oldest and favorite brother, Harry, failed to protect me.
Harry was staying in another apartment located in the same building with Mr. and Mrs. Merrill.

I felt ashamed and icky.
I didn't feel safe when my parents left me alone with him, but I couldn't say why.
I just begged them to please not leave me alone with Ian. They did.

My little five-year-old self had been forced to perform a sexual act against her will. She didn't even know what it was - all she knew was that she was afraid of him, so she did it.

I would call this "psychological terrorism."
I always felt terrorized by him after that.
My entire life.
It never happened again, but the damage was done.

To this day, I have trouble being "forced or coerced" into doing something.

I have forgiven him.
I have forgiven myself.
I am a survivor.
I am not a victim.

My prayer is for all five-year-olds to be able to keep their innocence.

- Anonymous

Dear Mamoni,

Hi!

I am your future self from 47 years later. As always, I have so much to say. Writing is a huge stimulant for me. Yet, I will try to keep it as short and sweet as possible.

This letter is not a lovey-dovey one for sure. I am not here to right any wrong. All I want in sharing my perspective is to allow healing to happen as a byproduct.

Each time you hurt; you rationalize by calling it a means to learn a life lesson. You justify your hurt by saying that surviving your worst helped you to help someone going through what you endured back then.

No one talks about or teaches how healing happens. The heart, or the feeling mind, stays open, gets hurt, and shuts down. The frayed fabric gets stitched over and over again in patches. Each stitch added a brick to build a barrier around the quaking heart to protect it from future hurt.

The thinking mind justified it as strengthening the soul, toughening up, etc. But what happened is each layer or barrier around the heart got calcified over time and thickened into a fortress.

The heart got imprisoned within itself.

Each time your eyes welled up; you dried up your unshed tears with a mighty speech of false bravado.

When your progressed sun moved into Pisces, your floodgates opened. You changed your professional career from an engineer to a hypnotherapist-healer.

The progressed sun is an astrological term. You were 45, then. It was right after your mom passed away.

In helping your clients find themselves, you have been finding yourself. Over time, we have grown closer. I feel good about it. As your clients heal, you heal.

Healing is a lifelong journey. And though it's lifelong, it doesn't need to take a lifetime to heal, sweet Mamoni.

Today, I come to you from way out in the future, from over four decades hence. I know it was rough then. Even now, you have triggers over unresolved issues.

Even when you didn't know why things were happening, you knew things were wrong; you felt violated. You were twelve when it happened the first time.

You just knew that things didn't feel right. You honored your feelings.

Trust me, you were tough, strong, and resilient, though you felt scared at home and on the streets. Those wanting to hurt you, a child both sensitive and innocent, were everywhere. You had nowhere to escape except within you.

I saw you; I was there with you. And I was always rooting for you.

You learned to go to bed with a pen knife under your pillow. You learned to walk around and travel with an open safety pin, always ready, between your thumb, forefinger, and middle finger.

You held the pin as if it were a writing instrument.

You know, Mamoni, those who hurt you could hurt you only once. That's both smart and wise.

Next time, you were ready to jab anyone who got near you with your pin or your knife. That was sheer courage!

You learned some men were leeches early on. They were wolves in sheep's clothes, filthy perverts in gentlemen's clothing who wouldn't spare a child if they could.

They never picked the loud and noisy kids. You were quiet and introverted, so they felt safe hurting you. And they did it once, and your unexpressed wrath was enough to get them the first time.

That's the universe working on your behalf.

You carried these deep battle wounds within you for all these years. When girls talked about surface-level stuff, you took pride in your wounds because what they dealt with wasn't even one-hundredth of what you had dealt with.

When someone shared their story of shame and violation, you knew why it was you who they felt comfortable talking about their troubles. They felt safe with you, and it was because you felt safe within you.

You had figured out that even your female elders could do nothing to help you. They were weak, too, trapped in their own stories of meek acceptance of patriarchy.

People talked, they cried, they laughed, they complained. But no one stood up and said, "That's ENOUGH!" out loud.

You were told this couldn't be true when you approached anyone with your story. And when anyone felt a flicker of truth, they asked you, "Shush!".

It wasn't fair then; it's not fair now. You found your way around. Since there was no fairness, you used forgiveness as your way out of that rotting hell, which grips men and women to prey on who they perceive as weaker than them.

You realized that you had to fight your fight on your own, and no one could be there for you. You became stronger than anyone you ever knew.

Your mental and emotional strength is unparalleled among anyone I have ever met. And you know this is true because I see you nod and smile as you read these words.

You are so strong that even the strongest people you meet in life, the spiritual teachers and mentors who are with you, lean on you to find their strength.

They hand over their work to you and ask you for favors.

Looking back, I see many have benefitted from associating with you. Everyone who is ever around you leaves feeling better.

You know you are an angel, a star seed, a light worker.

People have tried to blame and shame you for your sensitivity. Yet they took advantage of your sensitivity, unloaded their overloaded minds and overburdened hearts, and found solace in your company.

Now, isn't that ironic?

Over time, your protectors became your protectees.

Those who tried to hurt you looked at you for their relief.

Life truly reverses the game on you when you do the (spiritual) work when you heal.

When you heal, you help the transgressors heal.

Each time they hurt you, you fought back. Though you won, some of their energetic tentacles got hooked into you and kept you leaking energetically.

For years, you had no respite from the trauma of emotional and physical abuse and wounds from the past.

Your perpetrators had hurt you when you were a child and a teenager. But the pain lingered, the wounds festered for decades, and you carried it into your marriage and motherhood.

You could not free yourself from the puss oozing out of you until recently.

For over sixteen years, you have been practicing Ho'oponopono (the forgiveness ritual) daily. It's the not-commercial kind that everyone repeats as a mantra. For years, I have seen you get on your knees, stick your glutes to the ground, and do your daily ritual. That's discipline, dedication, and commitment.

You have kept your power and evolved because of your pain.

You blamed your mother for not siding with you. Yet, today, when you look back, you realize that she was always there with you.

You had to go through what you did because, without the pain, you would not have found your power or your peace. Your life wouldn't feel like poetry as it does today.

Even now, though your mom is dead and gone, you are stronger because of her. Her love has been an armor of strength that lets you take chances each day and remain curious.

Your mom needed security and certainty. She categorically told you, "Life isn't a gamble," when you told her it was so as you were leaving home to come to the USA as a 26-year-old.

Today, your entire life is a blessing for all the pain you endured from the early childhood hurts inflicted upon you by your "guardians."

It's never easy, yet you endured, you survived, you did not quit, and you lived through your mental, emotional, and physical agony. Today, you THRIVE!!!

The energetic feces from the past have served as fodder and have fueled your onward and upward journey to be the nearly mighty bamboo you are turning into, flexible yet tall, strong, and to some, come across as fearless.

You still have fears, and I know this is what makes you dare to take that next step in courage.

Each time you take that courageous step ahead, fear takes a step back.

Your memories that keep popping to the surface, reminding you of the (spiritual)work you need to do, keep you on this one-way upward solo hike through the canyons of your relationships, your business, and your life.

Most of the memories have faded. Those that remain have a neutral charge.

Being a clinical hypnotherapist, a trainer in neurolinguistic programming, and an energy medicine practitioner has helped you self-assess and self-heal.

I applaud your commitment to evolve and the side effects of the healing that has been happening along the way. You stopped blaming your abusers and started taking responsibility for the way you responded to your pain from the past. That created more pain, especially in your neck and shoulders.

The multiple car accidents are a byproduct of those festering traumas. Your failed marriage is also part of the collective wounding of your ancestors.

No one in your family knew a healthy, happy marriage, and you inherited their karma. Promiscuity is a norm; attempted incest is all part of your energetic heritage.

Your cells used to buzz with the wounds of both the abuser and the abused, the molester and the molested.

You cleaned up yourself. That helped your ancestors heal their wounds. Your healing yourself has helped your children and their children and the future generations of unborn ones heal.

Your journey is not one for the faint of heart. It takes a brave heart to heal ancestral trauma and take on the healing of the trauma of all of humanity.

Someone may challenge you and ask, "What do you mean by claiming you are healing humanity?" Here's what you can take on as the truth.

You heal yourself every day by taking your spiritual bath each morning, afternoon, evening, and night, keeping you clean and closer to light.

Your light lights up the world around you wherever you go. It helps the soul next to you breathe easier, smile wider and longer, and skip a step while walking.

Yes, you, my Mamoni, make this world a better place to live in by being in it.

The world is lighter because of you. There's less darkness and less heaviness where your light shows up and shines.

Thank you for never taking the thoughts of self-harm to fruition. Each time you thought you had no way out of your living hell except through death, I am glad you did not. Aren't you?

Look at all the lives you have touched over half a century. All the smiles you brought to many mouths are the rewards you get to reap for each time you thought of taking your life, and you didn't.

Once, at a Dale Carnegie class, you were asked what your magical power is. "The vanishing act" was your response! You were 33 then, yet all you wanted to do was vanish.

You are great at running away. I am glad you create new situations for yourself each time you move. I know you are not a tree, and thank God for that!

I love you very much and want you to continue standing up, speaking up, sharing, and shining. When you sparkle, you give others close to you permission to stand up, speak up, share, and shine.

Here's to many more decades of brilliance, darling Mamoni;

- Hugs and blessings,
Always your big sister, Keya-di

Keya Murthy, M.S., C.Ht. works as a Clinical Hypnotherapist, Spiritual Life Coach, and Energy Medicine Practitioner. She uses many tools to help her clients get closer to their core. That helps them find balance, peace, and harmony in their relationships and work life. Also, Keya is a #1 International Best-selling author and has published eleven books, which are available on Amazon and anywhere books are sold. She is also a sought out Trainer in Neurolinguistic Programming and Speaker.

You can reach her by writing to coaching@coachkeya.com

She sends out love notes and inspirational texts to her fans and followers.

You can subscribe to them for free at: https://coachkeya.com/newsletter/

For those on Facebook, join her free public group here: https://CoachKeya.com/Friend

For those on LinkedIn, connect with her at: https://www.linkedin.com/in/coachkeya/

For those on Instagram, follow her here: https://www.instagram.com/coachkeya/

For those on TikTok, follow her here: https://www.tiktok.com/@thecoachkeya

Subscribe to her YouTube channel here: https://www.youtube.com/coachkeya

Listen to The Be Happier Podcast with CoachKeya: http://bit.ly/behappierpodcast

I was seventeen.

I think I was home from college over the holiday break in the winter of 1984. I had met him during Sunday school and always crushed on him, which was mutual. We were older now, and I accepted when he invited me over to his place. His parents weren't home.

I told him up front that I didn't want to have sex – just fool around and that I wasn't prepared for sex - didn't have any birth control. Either he didn't hear me or didn't care. He finished inside me. Then gave me a plan B to take home with me. I didn't know what a "plan B" was or the horrible side effects I would experience later that night. It was painful enough that I had been violated, but what ensued was insult added to injury. He did not let me leave because one of his parents was home, and he didn't want them to know he had a girl in his room.

My mother was expecting me home and was very upset that I was late. I was hours late at this point, and when I got home, she was very angry. I was beside myself with worry. I called my best friend, Michelle. I didn't know why I was feeling so horrible. She suggested it was probably the Plan B and was horrified that he had date raped me. She knew him. I felt sick and nauseous with severe abdominal pain. I couldn't tell my mother.

I didn't tell her until many years later. I told her I was afraid to tell her because she was so angry that I was late. When I finally talked to her about the other date rape, she responded that my boyfriend at that time was good to "keep me." Unbelievable. That only added blame to my already complex and self-deprecating emotions.

Needless to say, I parent differently. My kids and I have an open dialogue about sex. I am grateful that this wounding has allowed me to be a better, more supportive parent. It took me many years to work through the shame. It is common for rape victims to blame themselves. It is NOT your fault. It didn't matter where you were or what you were wearing. You DID NOT ask for it. Rape is a crime of VIOLENCE. Not sex. It is carried out through sexual means, but it is, in fact, a crime of VIOLENCE.

- Jen Taylor

It was 2013, and I was in my early thirties. At the height of my career at the time, I was happy being without the weight of a heavy relationship and had been dating a man off and on for a little over a year. The relationship was extremely toxic, though, at the time, I don't think I cared too much. He was there when I needed someone or wanted good sex, and there was zero commitment. He was a largely known drug dealer and had a shady past, but I didn't ask anything about it. I honestly knew because people told me, but I pretended I didn't know. As long as it didn't involve me, I figured we could lead separate lives and just get what each of us wanted from the relationship instead of trying to complicate things.

Sure, he cheated on me. Sure, he did drugs. Sure, there was a rumor he was married or separated. I was not sure of any of it. I left his life alone and let myself get lost in a good time when we were together. I had an extremely stressful career, so I didn't have much time to enjoy myself. When I met E, I let myself have fun when I was with him. We didn't really have a relationship status for ourselves. We had met each other's friends, kids, and relatives. We worked together for a while and traveled for a whole year all around the country with work to sell cars. When on the road, it was a huge party, with lots of drugs and alcohol. I didn't do drugs, and I rarely drank on the road. I was the only woman in a group of about twelve men. So, I actually acted as if I was responsible for all of them. Not being in a serious relationship was good for me, and without a title, I was free to be myself in most ways.

I don't recall E ever being controlling. As a matter of fact, the five years we spent off and on, I can probably count on one hand the times we actually fought. We were a pretty laid-back couple, and while everyone knew we were a couple, we weren't at the same time. It wasn't long before I started to drink heavily because of the crowd I hung with and E's influence. It was only time, and I began to smoke weed. I wasn't one to do anything more than that because drugs had always scared me. It took a long time before I would even do weed. E was protective of me and always told me I had to smoke what he gave me and never anything else. He was adamant that other people could lace the weed with something, and he warned me never to smoke something that he hadn't checked out or given me. I trusted him. As a matter of fact, in a crazy way, he gave me the security and companionship I craved.

E always called me his angel and often would refer to me as heaven-sent. He would joke I was too good for him and treated me well for us not to be really anything. He would help me with a bill if needed, and I would do the same for him. One of the things I loved most about him was that he would often sing to me. He had a great voice, and many years before he threw away his life to drug dealing, he sang in a group. He was always kind to me, and since I could be strongly opinionated, he would often tell me it was in a way that I had never had a man do to me. He was not angry, but he stood up to me, and men didn't often do that because I was intimidating to most men with my independence.

Sex with E was always great, and the kind of passionate sex that usually drives you back to someone over and over, even if you know the relationship isn't healthy. Many times, during our off-and-on status, I would date other people, and often, he would ask to meet up, but if I were dating someone in a committed way, I would always tell him I couldn't do that. I would meet him for lunch or drinks, but sex was off the table. While he gave me a hard time and often begged regardless, he never pressured me to do anything I didn't want to do. If I said no, it was no, and he would beg or pout but leave me be. Deep down, I always thought he probably respected me for that because he knew I didn't mess around when I was with him. I just wasn't that kind of gal. During the five years of being off and on, I serial dated and never stayed with a man very long. So, if I pushed E away, he knew it was only weeks and I would be back. I wasn't ready to be committed, and most men were not what I wanted. E always respected me and my boundaries until he didn't.

The first time he didn't respect my boundaries started in a small way. He brought a friend to my house one night, and he took me into the bedroom to have sex. While we were having sex, he called out to his friend, and he came in there. E told me to perform oral sex on him while he finished having sex with me. I told him I didn't want to do that, and before I could say anything else, his friend was inside my mouth. I came from a strict, patriarchal family, and obedience was something I did or was punished for. I remember displacing myself somewhere else, and finally, they both finished. He even wouldn't let me spit it out. I remember thinking I was so glad it was over and how unlike E it was for him to make me do this. E casually kissed me and praised me for being a good girl that he could show off. He mentioned owing the friend money and that I was more than enough to cover it. Everything was so cloudy that it took days before I processed that remark to realize he had trafficked me in a sick sort of way.

I was so ashamed, and I felt like I couldn't tell anyone. The family I was raised in taught me that if a woman is raped that she brought it upon herself with what she was wearing, her makeup being too heavy, or flirting when she shouldn't, so I assumed it was my fault. I finally told E that I didn't want him ever to do that again and that it made me feel awful. He was nice and told me he understood, but his friend loved it and wanted to meet again. I just said no.

Months went by, and he honored his word. He didn't do it again. I felt safe again, and maybe it had just been a misunderstanding. Perhaps I had misled him into thinking I wanted to do those things. I took the blame. Then, one night, we were out on the road traveling when he invited another friend to "do whatever he wanted to me" while he went downstairs to take care of some drug business. The friend was nice and told me he wasn't going to do that to me after E left the room. He asked me why I was with someone like that and told me I could do better. We sat there and talked. When E came back, the guy left, and E bragged again about how much he showed me off, but I never told him that the guy didn't take advantage of me because I was afraid he would be upset. Instead, when we got back home, I found another job and cut contact with him.

It stayed that way for months, and then my best friend at the time called me to let me know he had met E for lunch. He told me how he had cried to him and told him he had messed up with me. He begged him to try to talk me into unblocking him so he could talk to me. He went on about how he loved me and how torn up he was, so I reluctantly unblocked him so he could call. When E called, he told me he was sorry and shouldn't have done anything to make me feel bad. He told me he had been having a hard time and wanted to meet. I agreed. I missed him, and I hoped he understood that I was serious about not wanting him to "showcase" me with his friends or colleagues.

Things went much better, and E kept his word. He said he was afraid he had lost me for good. He didn't pressure me or ask me to do anything I didn't want to do. It was like old times; I was so happy again with us being us. I started to trust him again and the ability he could change. As a matter of fact, during that year, he had made sure he treated me like a queen. If I didn't want to do something or said no, he respected that. We were off and on still, but only pausing things when I had a boyfriend and wouldn't cheat.

Then I met a guy that I started dating steadily and rather seriously. Months went by, and I brushed E off for any of his usual begging for sex. I avoided contacting him because

I knew he wasn't happy with me finally dating someone longer than a couple of weeks. One night, it was late, and E kept trying to call me. I kept pushing it to voicemail because I was avoiding him, and my boyfriend was at my house that night. Finally, he texted me and told me it was an emergency and that he wanted me to come to his store in town because he needed to talk to me. My toxic pull on him was strong, so I told my boyfriend at the time I needed to go somewhere for a short time, and I went to see E at his store. When I went in, the store was dark and closed. He was sitting on the back couch and drinking whiskey. I could tell he was a bit wasted because he was all up in his feelings, and he usually only did that when he had drunk too much. He begged me to take a few shots, and I knew better; brown liquor made me black out pockets of time, and I would only do it with people I felt safe with usually. I was shaking from the liquor starting to get into my system, so he rolled me a joint and pushed me a pill, telling me it was for anxiety. I took the pill and then took a couple of hits on the joint. Before I knew it, I felt spacy and as if I could see what was going on around me but not respond. Loopy.

I think I drifted in and out of the loopy existence because pockets of time seem to be missing, and I only remember glitchy moments from the experience. I remember several of his friends' faces. Maybe five or six of them. All of them smelled heavy with liquor. They touched me, forced sex on me, and even took pictures and videos of me. They told me I was enjoying it and a bad girl. I remember thinking it felt good, but yet I was scared and like I wanted to stop it, but I didn't have the words to say or the thought capacity to do so from the liquor or drugs. They finally left me to wake up on the cold concrete in the back room in the wee hours of the morning. My boyfriend had tried to call my phone many times and finally left a message breaking up with me. I was shaking, cold, and sick.

I went home and am shocked even today that I drove home in my condition. I took a shower and tried to scrub the memory and smell off me. I would later find out they drugged me, and it was the last time I met him in private. I was scared to tell anyone because I didn't know if I told them they could in my state of disillusion. I don't remember so much. Finally, one day, I broke down and told my best friend when he encouraged me to call E to make up. I told him E wasn't who he thought he was and that he gave me to his friends for sex and traded me for money he owed people. I didn't know if he would believe me, but I was ready to tell someone. I remember him being quiet on the phone and telling me he had to go. I thought I had ruined our friendship, and he didn't believe me. Later, I found out he called E and threatened him never to touch me or put me in a wrong position ever again. He told him to leave me alone and never talk to me. He was so angry. I felt so much better that someone thought it was wrong and took up for me in a way I felt like I couldn't for myself. He never mentioned it to me again except when he told me to stay away from E.

Now, when someone forces me to do things or even asks me to do certain sexual acts, I have severe flashbacks to that moment. I have even broken up with men since then because sex felt terrible, and I felt forced to do things. It has been a long road of recovery. E is in prison for unrelated charges, and I haven't had contact with him in a long time, but the memory is still there. I have taken my time to educate my kids that they can like certain sexual activities and still be careful of boundaries in which they do not feel safe. I am not sure that there is an answer to healing. I still deal with a lot from the experience, but I do know that I do not put myself in any position where I do not feel safe anymore, even something as simple as a party feeling unsafe or a specific hotel. I get out of the situation the moment my internal radar alerts me. I might be over-reactive, but I would rather be that than ever face those memories again.

Stay safe. Listen to your internal radar. If you say no or are unable to consent, it is wrong. You didn't do anything to deserve it. They violated you and your boundaries. Period.

Healing sometimes comes on a day-by-day basis. That is okay. You might never be the same or okay, but that is okay, too. You have the right to hurt, heal, and choose your own path from the tragic trauma. I am sending you all my love as you heal.

- Anonymous

MESSAGES OF HOPE

We collected some messages from those who have struggled with self-harm and suicide on:

"What help/advice can you offer someone who is going through a similar situation?"

Here were their unedited answers to messages of hope they wanted to share with you:

Take a deep breath. Now take another one. Continue to take deep breaths. Sometimes that's all you can do, just breathe. There is no perfect formula for healing. No real guidebook on how to process and move on. You don't have to be completely okay again. You choose your timeline. You make the decisions. You, no one else. You process, you adjust, you breath on your own terms. Eventually, hopefully, one day, you'll be able to breath without fear. "Your healing cannot depend on the other person admitting the damage that they have caused you. Because more often than not, they won't admit it. It is entirely on you to heal what they broke in you."

~ Kayil York

Find safety first. Then seek help. It's difficult to weed through thoughts that are disguised at best.

Find your path to healing, get support, know you might never fully heal, and all of that is okay. Your path to healing gets to be cloudy. You did not ask for it. It is not your fault.

APPENDIX ON SUPPORT RESOURCES & CHOICES

Includes Links, Numbers, & Resources For Sexual Assault, Rape, Incest, and Pregnancy Choices

In my letter, I described how, at 17, I was date raped in college, and I got pregnant. Unfortunately, I didn't really know what to do. I didn't know about Plan B and didn't go to the hospital. I was in shock and alone in my experience. Later, I did talk to my mother, and she, thankfully, set me up with a gynecologist, who terminated the pregnancy from the date rape. Ironically, he would deliver my son years later.

Abortion had been legal in 49 U.S. States with Roe v. Wade. Once R v W was overturned, abortion access varied state-by-state. Planned Parenthood has a link to check your state's laws:

Where is Abortion Illegal? | Abortion Limits by State

Thankfully, legislation is being passed for an over-the-counter birth control pill. "Opill" is going to hit pharmacies so that if one needs birth control, they can grab it off the shelf and go to the pharmacist with their insurance cards and get a prescription for it right there. This way, the insurance company is covering the cost.

United States Resources:

If you or someone you know is experiencing sexual assault, rape, or incest - please reach out 24/7 to the following:

National Sexual Assault Hotline: 800 656 HOPE
or www.rainn.org
(Rape, abuse, and incest national hotline)

National Domestic Violence Hotline: 800 787 7233
or www.thehotline.org

Planned Parenthood Hotline: 800 230 7526
or www.plannedparenthood.org

Find support.

- Jen Taylor, LCSW

APPENDIX ON SUICIDE RESOURCES

**Includes Resources for
Suicide Help & Assessment**

List of Suicide Help & Hotlines[1]:
(United States and Worldwide)

United States:
Emergency: 911
Suicide Hotline: 988

Algeria:
Emergency: 34342 and 43
Suicide Hotline: 0021 3983 2000 58

Angola:
Emergency: 113

Argentina:
Emergency: 911
Suicide Hotline: 135

Armenia:
Emergency: 911 and 112
Suicide Hotline: (2) 538194

---

[1] List of Helplines and Hotline Numbers Retrieved from blog.opencounseling.com

Australia:
Emergency: 000
Suicide Hotline: 131114

Austria:
Emergency: 112
Telefonseelsorge 24/7 142
Rat auf Draht 24/7 147 (Youth)

Bahamas:
Emergency: 911
Suicide Hotline: (2) 322-2763

Bahrain:
Emergency: 999

Bangladesh:
Emergency: 999

Barbados:
Emergency: 911
Suicide Hotline Samaritan Barbados: (246) 4299999

Belgium:
Emergency: 112
Suicide Hotline Stichting Zelfmoordlijn: 1813

Bolivia:
Emergency: 911
Suicide Hotline: 3911270

Bosnia & Herzegovina:
Suicide Hotline: 080 05 03 05

Botswana:
Emergency: 911
Suicide Hotline: +2673911270

Brazil:
Emergency: 188

Bulgaria:
Emergency: 112
Suicide Hotline: 0035 9249 17 223

Burundi:
Emergency: 117

Burkina Faso:
Emergency: 17

Canada:
Emergency: 911
Suicide Hotline: 1 (822) 456 4566

Chad:
Emergency: 2251-1237

China:
Emergency: 110
Suicide Hotline: 800-810-1117

Columbia:
24/7 Helpline in Barranquilla: 1(00 57 5) 372 27 27
24/7 Hotline Bogota: (57-1 323 24 25

Congo:
Emergency: 117

Costa Rica:
Emergency: 911
Suicide Hotline: 506-253-5439

Croatia:
Emergency: 112

Cyprus:
Emergency: 112
Suicide Hotline: 8000 7773

Czech Republic:
Emergency: 112

Denmark:
Emergency: 112
Suicide Hotline: 4570201201

Dominican Republic:
Emergency: 911
Suicide Hotline: (809) 562-3500

Ecuador:
Emergency: 911

Egypt:
Emergency: 122
Suicide Hotline: 131114

El Salvador:
Emergency: 911
Suicide Hotline: 126

Equatorial Guinea:
Emergency: 114

Estonia:
Emergency:112
Suicide Hotline: 3726558088
In Russian: 3726555688

Ethiopia:
Emergency: 911

Finland:
Emergency: 112
Suicide Hotline: 010 195 202

France:
Emergency: 112
Suicide Hotline: 0145394000

Germany:
Emergency: 112
Suicide Hotline: 0800 111 0 111

Ghana:
Emergency: 999
Suicide Hotline: 2332 444 71279

Greece:
Emergency: 1018

Guatemala:
Emergency: 110
Suicide Hotline: 5392-5953

Guinea:
Emergency: 117

Guinea Bissau:
Emergency: 117

Guyana:
Emergency: 999
Suicide Hotline: 223-0001

Holland:
Suicide Hotline: 09000767

Hong Kong:
Emergency: 999
Suicide Hotline: 852 2382 0000

Hungary:
Emergency: 112
Suicide Hotline: 116123

India:
Emergency: 112
Suicide Hotline: 8888817666

Indonesia:
Emergency: 112
Suicide Hotline: 1-800-273-8255

Iran:
Emergency: 110
Suicide Hotline: 1480

Ireland:
Emergency: 116123
Suicide Hotline: +4408457909090

Israel:
Emergency: 100
Suicide Hotline: 1201

Italy:
Emergency: 112
Suicide Hotline: 800860022

Jamaica:
Suicide Hotline: 1-888-429-KARE (5273)

Japan:
Emergency: 110
Suicide Hotline: 810352869090

Jordan:
Emergency: 911
Suicide Hotline: 110

Kenya:
Emergency: 999
Suicide Hotline: 722178177

Kuwait:
Emergency: 112
Suicide Hotline: 94069304

Latvia:
Emergency: 113
Suicide Hotline: 371 67222922

Lebanon:
Suicide Hotline: 1564

Liberia:
Emergency: 911
Suicide Hotline: 6534308

Luxembourg:
Emergency: 112
Suicide Hotline: 352 45 45 45

Madagascar:
Emergency: 117

Malaysia:
Emergency: 999
Suicide Hotline: (06) 2842500

Mali:
Emergency: 8000-1115

Malta:
Suicide Hotline: 179

Mauritius:
Emergency: 112
Suicide Hotline: +230 800 93 93

Mexico:
Emergency: 911
Suicide Hotline: 5255102550

Netherlands:
Emergency: 112
Suicide Hotline: 900 0113

New Zealand:
Emergency: 111
Suicide Hotline: 1737

Niger:
Emergency: 112

Nigeria:
Suicide Hotline: 234 8092106493

Norway:
Emergency: 112
Suicide Hotline: +4781533300

Pakistan:
Emergency: 115

Peru:
Emergency: 911
Suicide Hotline: 381-3695

Philippines:
Emergency: 911
Suicide Hotline: 028969191

Poland:
Emergency: 112
Suicide Hotline: 5270000

Portugal:
Emergency: 112
Suicide Hotline: 21 854 07 40
And 8 96 898 21 50

Qatar:
Emergency: 999

Romania:
Emergency: 112
Suicide Hotline: 0800 801200

Russia:
Emergency: 112
Suicide Hotline: 0078202577577

Saint Vincent and the Grenadines:
Suicide Hotline: 9784 456 1044

São Tomé and Príncipe:
Suicide Hotline: (239) 222-12-22 ext. 123

Saudi Arabia:
Emergency: 112

Serbia:
Suicide Hotline: (+381) 21-6623-393

Senegal:
Emergency: 17

Singapore:
Emergency: 999
Suicide Hotline: 1 800 2214444

Spain:
Emergency: 112
Suicide Hotline: 914590050

South Africa:
Emergency: 10111
Suicide Hotline: 0514445691

South Korea:
Emergency: 112
Suicide Hotline: (02) 7158600

Sri Lanka:
Suicide Hotline: 011 057 2222662

Sudan:
Suicide Hotline: (249) 11-555-253

Sweden:
Emergency: 112
Suicide Hotline: 46317112400

Switzerland:
Emergency: 112
Suicide Hotline: 143

Tanzania:
Emergency: 112

Thailand:
Suicide Hotline: (02) 713-6793

Tonga:
Suicide Hotline: 23000

Trinidad and Tobago:
Suicide Hotline: (868) 645 2800

Tunisia:
Emergency: 197

Turkey:
Emergency: 112

Uganda:
Emergency: 112
Suicide Hotline: 0800 21 21 21

United Arab Emirates:
Suicide Hotline: 800 46342

United Kingdom:
Emergency: 112
Suicide Hotline: 0800 689 5652

United States:
Emergency: 911
Suicide Hotline: 988

Zambia:
Emergency: 999
Suicide Hotline: +260960264040

Zimbabwe:
Emergency: 999
Suicide Hotline: 080 12 333 333

CONDUCT A SUICIDE INQUIRY[2]

a. Ideation

Frequency, Intensity and Duration

- Have you had thoughts of hurting yourself or others?
- Have you thought about ending your life?

Now, in the Past, and at its Worst

- During the last 48 hours, past month, and worst ever: How much? How intense? Lasting for how long?

b. Plan

Timing, Location, Lethality, Availability/Means

- When you think about killing yourself or ending your life, what do you imagine?
- When? Where? How would you do it? In what way?

---

[2] Retrieved from Minnesota Department of Health at: https://www.health.state.mn.us/people/syringe/suicide.pdf

Preparatory Acts

- What steps have you taken to prepare to kill yourself, if any?

c. Behavior

Past attempts, aborted attempts, rehearsals

- Have you ever thought about or tried to kill yourself in the past?
- Have you ever taken any actions to rehearse or practice ending your life (e.g., tying noose, loading gun, measuring substance)?

Non-suicidal self-injurious behavior

- Are you having paranoid thoughts? Hallucinations?
- Have you done anything to hurt yourself (e.g., cutting, burning or mutilation)?

d. Intent

Extent to which they expect to carry out the plan and believe the plan to be lethal versus harmful.

- What do you think will happen?
- What things put you at risk of ending your life or

killing yourself (reasons to die)?
- What things prevent you from killing yourself and keep you safe (reasons to live)?

Explore ambivalence between reasons to die and reasons to live. Pay attention to how they describe the outcome.

- "I'm dead, it's over." indicates a higher risk of suicide death.
- "I think I'd end up in the hospital." indicates a moderate risk of suicide death.
- "I don't want to die; I want my suffering to end." indicates a lower risk of suicide death.

e. Notes

- When working with **youth**, collect information from a parent, guardian or service provider on the youth's suicidal thoughts, plans, behaviors, and changes in mood, behavior or disposition.
- If the person has thoughts or plans to **harm someone else**, conduct a homicide inquiry using the same questions (replace "hurt or kill yourself" with "hurt or kill someone else").

DETERMINE RISK LEVEL[3]

The risk level is determined with the previous three steps:
1. Risk Factors
2. Protective Factors
3. Suicide Inquiry

Death by Suicide Risk Level

Risk Level	Risk Factors	Protective Factors	Suicide Inquiry	Intervention*
High	Multiple risk factors	Protective factors are not present or not relevant at this time	Potentially lethal suicide attempt or persistent ideation with strong intent or suicide rehearsal	Hospital admission generally indicated, suicide precautions (e.g., observation, means reduction)
Moderate	Multiple risk factors	Few protective factors	Suicidal ideation with a plan, but not intent or behavior	Hospital admission may be necessary, develop crisis plan and suicide precautions, give emergency/crisis numbers

---

[3] Retrieved from Minnesota Department of Health at: https://www.health.state.mn.us/people/syringe/suicide.pdf

| Low | Few and/or modifiable risk factors | Strong protective factors | Thoughts of death with no plan, intent or behavior | Outpatient referral, symptom reduction, give emergency/crisis numbers |

Take every suicide attempt seriously!

People often think a person is not really suicidal.

It's better to be safe, even if they will be angry with you for taking action to keep them alive.

ABOUT THE AUTHOR

Jen Taylor, LCSW
#1 International Bestselling Author

Jen Taylor, LCSW is a New York-based spiritual psychotherapist with 23+ years of experience. Jen specializes in womens' empowerment, domestic violence, teens, and LGBTQIA+ individuals. Jen incorporates spirituality and astrology into her sessions to create a truly unique blend of guidance.

Jen was born and raised in New York City and lived there from preschool through high school. Instead of attending her prom, Jen went to boot camp for the Navy and received accreditation as a U.S. Naval photographer. Jen then received her Bachelor's in Arts from Haverford College in Pennsylvania and studied abroad in Florence, Italy. She spent her early 20s in the advertising office of Italian *Vogue* and went on to attend social work school at Fordham University's Graduate school of social services. In 1999, Jen received her Master's in social work while pregnant with her first child, Giancarlo. Jen worked in various outpatient mental health clinics in New York City, and in 2007 had her second child, Elisabetta.

Jen Taylor, LCSW is the editor for Girl on Fire Magazine's "Wine Down with Jen," where she uses her 20+ years of experience as a New York-based spiritual psychotherapist to bring you cozy couch conversations you would have with your best friend over a glass of wine after work.

When not writing for the magazine or seeing clients, Jen enjoys traveling, photography, spending time with her kids, and a good cup of coffee.

Jen is a multiple #1 International bestselling author in a collaboration series and currently working on releasing the rest of this series as her very first solo books over the next year.

To connect with Jen, she can be reached at Jentaylorfani@gmail.com

www.ingramcontent.com/pod-product-compliance
Lightning Source LLC
LaVergne TN
LVHW010606070526
838199LV00063BA/5090